PEOPLE AT
THE CENTER OF

THE CIVIL WAR

By CHRIS HUGHES

BLACKBIRCH™
PRESS

THOMSON

GALE

San Diego • Detroit • New York • San Francisco • Cleveland
New Haven, Conn. • Waterville, Maine • London • Munich

THOMSON
GALE

LIBRARY OF CONGRESS CATALOGING-IN-PUBLICATION DATA

Hughes, Christopher (Christopher A.), 1968-
  The Civil War / by Chris Hughes.
    p. cm. — (People at the center of:)
  Includes bibliographical references and index.
  Contents: The United States Civil War — John Caldwell Calhoun (1782-1850) —Dred
Scott (c.1800 - 1858) — Ulysses Simpson Grant (1822-1885) — William Tecumseh Sherman
(1820-1891).
   ISBN 1-56711-764-3
   1. United States—History—Civil War, 1861-1865—Biography—Juvenile literature. [1.
United States—History—Civil War,1861-1865—Biography.] I. Title. II. Series.

  E467.H886 2004
  973.7'092'2—dc21
                                                                  2003003621

CONTENTS

THE CIVIL WAR

"The hoarse and indistinguishable orders of commanding officers, the screaming and bursting of shells, canister and shrapnel as they tore through the struggling masses of humanity, the death screams of wounded animals, the groans of their human companions, wounded and dying and trampled underfoot by hurrying batteries, riderless horses and the moving lines of battle . . . a perfect hell on earth, never, perhaps, to be equaled, certainly not to be surpassed, nor ever to be forgotten in a man's lifetime."

A former Civil War soldier recorded these memories fifty years after the war ended. Although this soldier was describing the events at the battle of Gettysburg in 1863, he could have been describing many of the battles between the North and the South from 1861 to 1865. More American soldiers were killed in the Civil War than in any other war. The Civil War divided northern states from southern states, split some states apart, and sometimes caused friends and family members to fight against one another.

Since colonial times, the North and South had grown in different directions. The warm climate of the South was perfect for large plantations that grew crops such as rice, tobacco, and cotton. Slaves provided the hard work these crops required. The North developed factories, most of the nation's large cities, and advances in transportation and communication.

Conflicts began to emerge between the industrialized North and the agricultural South because of these differences. Southerners thought that slavery was crucial to the survival of their economy. After Eli Whitney invented the cotton gin in 1793, it became possible for southern plantations to make huge profits by using slaves to grow cotton, which was then sold to Europe. Slaves were not needed in the North, and growing numbers of abolitionists who wanted to end slavery began to voice their opinions.

The Battle of Gettysburg was a destructive and bloody event that survivors remembered for the rest of their lives.

A.Walker, 1883.

Another division between the North and South involved the rights of the individual states. The South wanted each state to be able to control its own affairs, especially in the areas of trade, taxes, and slavery. The North wanted the federal government to have a more central role in those decisions and the states to be bound by the decisions of the government.

Although Congress attempted to make a series of compromises between northern and southern interests, the two sides continued to grow apart. The biggest questions involved whether slavery would be allowed in territories, which were areas that were not yet states. In 1848, the United States defeated Mexico after a two-year war, and gained land that would become the states of California, Arizona, New Mexico, Nevada, Utah, and part of Colorado. This new territory increased the tensions between North and South over those questions of slavery and the role of the federal

The success of Southern cotton plantations, like the one depicted here, depended on the work of slaves. Slavery became a central issue of the Civil War.

government. In 1857, the Supreme Court declared that Congress did not have the right to decide whether a territory or state would allow slavery. By then, there seemed to be no way for the North and the South to work together peacefully.

In the presidential election of 1860, the Democratic Party was divided between Southern Democrats and Northern Democrats. Republicans banded together behind Abraham Lincoln, who was opposed to the spread of slavery. With the Democrats divided, Lincoln won the election. Fearful that Lincoln would eventually end slavery, South Carolina decided to secede, or withdraw, from the United States. Six other

In the first major battle of the Civil War, the Battle of Bull Run, Confederate troops clashed with the more numerous Union forces and emerged victorious.

Southern states soon followed. These seven states formed the Confederate States of America and chose Jefferson Davis as their president.

The first military clash between the Confederacy and the Union (as the North was called) took place near Charleston, South Carolina, on April 12, 1861. There, Union soldiers defended Fort Sumter. Lincoln had to decide whether to send supplies to the fort or abandon it; the Confederates in South Carolina declared that they would attack if the fort was not abandoned. When Lincoln sent the supplies. Confederate forces opened fire on the fort and forced the men inside to surrender.

In 1861, four more states seceded from the Union. Virginia was one of those states, and Richmond became the Confederate capital. In July 1861, Confederate forces met Union troops along a stream called Bull Run at Manassas Junction in Virginia, and engaged in the war's first major battle. Though outnumbered, the Confederates won this battle.

After Bull Run, the conflict expanded quickly. In early 1862, Confederate general "Stonewall" Jackson defeated Union forces in Virginia's Shenandoah Valley. Union general George McClellan tried to capture Richmond but was turned back in June as General Robert E. Lee took command of the Virginia armies. Lee followed this with another Confederate victory at Bull Run.

Also in 1862, the battles of Shiloh in Tennessee, Antietam in Maryland, and Fredericksburg in Virginia combined to produce more than sixty-three thousand casualties. Following Antietam, Lincoln issued his Emancipation Proclamation. This document declared that all slaves in states that were still fighting against the Union as of the end of that year would be free. The Emancipation Proclamation turned the focus of the war from a fight about states' rights to a fight over slavery. Nations in Europe, many of whom favored the South because of the cotton trade, were not willing to enter a war to protect slavery.

The next year brought a Confederate victory at Chancellorsville, Virginia, followed by two critical Union victories: at Vicksburg along the Mississippi River and at Gettysburg in Pennsylvania. In 1864, Union general Ulysses S.

John Wilkes Booth assassinated President Abraham Lincoln at Ford's Theater just days after the end of the war.

Grant was brought east from Vicksburg by Lincoln. Lincoln wanted a general who would push Lee hard enough to end the war. With a brutal campaign throughout 1864 and into 1865, which included William T. Sherman's destructive march through Georgia and South Carolina, the Union defeated the Confederacy. On April 9, 1865, Lee surrendered to Grant at Appomattox Court House in Virginia.

What remained was for the nation to find a way to heal itself and reunite. That hope was damaged less than a week after Lee's surrender, when John Wilkes Booth assassinated Lincoln in Washington. With more than six hundred thousand men killed, immeasurable damage done to the land on which huge armies had battled, and uncertain leadership, it took the nation a long time to become whole and healthy again. When it finally did, the United States emerged from the Civil War stronger and more united than ever before.

JOHN C. CALHOUN

John C. Calhoun was born in 1782 near Abbeville, South Carolina. Calhoun was mostly self-educated until he entered Yale College in Connecticut in 1801. He later became a lawyer. In 1811, he was elected to the U.S. House of Representatives.

In 1817, Calhoun became President James Monroe's secretary of war. He was elected vice president under John Quincy Adams in 1824, and when Andrew Jackson defeated Adams in the 1828 election, Calhoun again was elected vice president.

Jackson supported a strong tariff, or tax on imports, that hurt southern cotton growers. Calhoun wrote a paper called the "South Carolina Exposition and Protest," in which he claimed that a state had the right to nullify, or ignore, a federal law that violated the Constitution. Calhoun argued that the tariff was unconstitutional and unfairly favored northern factories over southern growers. Unable to influence Jackson, Calhoun resigned as vice president. In 1832, he was elected to the Senate.

Above: Entire families of slaves toiled in southern cotton fields. Right: John C. Calhoun held many influential political offices and was a strong advocate of states' rights, which included the right to allow slavery.

As senator, Calhoun pushed for a tariff more favorable to the South, and from that point on was marked by his desire to protect the South, the cotton industry, and slavery, from the North. He served as secretary of state for President John Tyler in 1844, and he helped arrange for the United States to annex Texas, which brought another slave state into the Union. In 1845, Calhoun returned to the Senate, where he continued to oppose any attempts to limit the spread of slavery. Calhoun died days after making an argument on this point in 1850.

Best known as a supporter of states' rights, including the right to allow slavery, Calhoun acted in what he believed were the best interests of the nation as a whole. He was convinced that any attempt by the federal government to limit slavery or control the states would lead to a division of the Union. Ten years later, he was proved correct. Calhoun's views helped justify secession in 1860.

HARRIET BEECHER STOWE

AUTHOR, EDUCATOR INSPIRED ABOLITIONISTS

Born in Connecticut in 1811, Harriet Beecher Stowe was the seventh child of a minister, Lyman Beecher, who was an abolitionist. Harriet's older sister, Catherine, took charge of her education after their mother died in 1815. Harriet was well educated, and she became a strong opponent of slavery and an active supporter of women's rights.

Convinced that education was the key to reform. Harriet became a teacher and began to write educational books and magazine articles. In 1836, she married Calvin Stowe, a professor in Cincinnati, where she first came into direct contact with slavery.

Stowe's most famous book is *Uncle Tom's Cabin*, a story about life as a slave that openly portrays the evils of slavery. By the end of the book's first year in print, three hundred thousand copies had been sold in America and another two hundred thousand in England. It was also translated into several other languages.

Uncle Tom's Cabin was published at a time when tensions were high between the North and South, and slavery was an explosive issue. Many Southerners who supported slavery condemned the book. Abolitionists used it to point out the injustice of slavery, and the book turned people against slavery who had never considered the question before. It brought widespread attention to one of the major differences between the North and South, which pushed the two sides farther apart than ever.

Stowe went on to write many other books, and

PRICE $1.00 FOR TWO VOLS.—VOL. I.

UNCLE TOM'S CABIN;

OR,

LIFE AMONG THE LOWLY.

BY

HARRIET BEECHER STOWE.

BOSTON:
PUBLISHED BY JOHN P. JEWETT & CO.
CLEVELAND, OHIO:
JEWETT, PROCTOR & WORTHINGTON.
1852.

Harriet Beecher Stowe (left) expressed her abolitionist views in Uncle Tom's Cabin *(above). The controversial book openly portrayed the evils of slavery.*

she became one of the most famous American authors of her time. Nothing else Stowe wrote, however, had the impact of *Uncle Tom's Cabin*. When he met her in 1862, Abraham Lincoln said, "So, you are the little woman who wrote the book that started this great war!" Stowe died in 1896.

FREDERICK DOUGLASS

Born Frederick Augustus Washington Bailey around 1817, Frederick Douglass was raised by his grandmother on a plantation near Tuckahoe, Maryland. At about eight years of age, Douglass was sent to work in a house in Baltimore, where the wife of his master secretly taught him to read and write. Douglass later served as a slave at the docks in Baltimore. In 1838, he was able to escape on board a northbound ship; he changed his name to Frederick Douglass to avoid capture. Douglass married a free woman named Anna Murray, and they settled in Massachusetts.

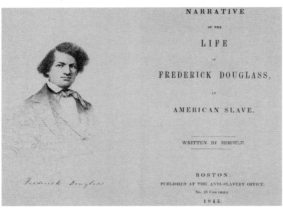

Above: Frederick Douglass published several books about his life as a slave. Right: Douglass was a passionate speaker and writer who insisted that President Lincoln abolish slavery.

In 1841, newspaper editor William Lloyd Garrison enlisted Douglass as a speaker for Garrison's Anti-Slavery Society. Soon Douglass made speeches throughout the North. In 1845. Douglass published *Narrative of the Life of Frederick Douglass*, the first of several books about his life as a slave. From 1845 until 1847, Douglass lived in England, where he continued to speak against slavery.

In 1847, Douglass returned to the United States. His supporters had purchased his freedom, so he was safe from slave catchers. In Rochester, New York, Douglass began his own newspaper called the *North Star*, which he used to argue for the abolition of slavery and rights for free blacks.

When the Civil War began, Douglass pressured President Abraham Lincoln to free the slaves. He argued that it would serve the military needs of the Union as well as the goals of the abolitionists, since African American troops could be used in the Union army. Through his newspaper and his speeches, Douglass was one of the people responsible for making the Civil War a war against slavery and not simply a war about states' rights.

After the war, Douglass remained a public figure. He served in various political roles in Washington, D.C., and worked hard for equal rights for blacks and for women until his death in 1895.

HARRIET TUBMAN

Araminta Ross was born a slave in Maryland around 1821; later she took her mother's name, Harriet. One of eleven children, she grew up working in the fields and the house of her masters. While she was still a child, her master struck her in the head, and for the rest of her life she endured seizures.

In 1844, Harriet married John Tubman. Five years later, she left her husband, parents, and siblings behind and fled to Philadelphia. There, she began to organize the escapes of her family and other slaves (her husband, who was free, remarried and stayed behind). Some historians estimate that Harriet Tubman helped three hundred slaves escape through what was known as the Underground Railroad, a network of antislavery contacts, friends, and escape routes that hid slaves from slave catchers. In Maryland, a reward of forty thousand dollars was offered for her capture.

When the Civil War began, Tubman was already famous as a "conductor" on the Underground

As a conductor on the Underground Railroad, Harriet Tubman (left) led hundreds of escaped slaves through a network of safe houses, like the one in the photo above.

Railroad and as an antislavery speaker. Her work had helped turn slavery into one of the main issues of the Civil War. In 1862 she began work as a nurse in South Carolina. At the same time, she served as a spy for the Union forces and she used her own network of friends and hiding places to gain information about Confederate plans.

Known to many as "Moses," Tubman was known and respected by such leading abolitionists as Frederick Douglass, an escaped slave and famous speaker. Douglass once wrote to her, "Excepting John Brown . . . I know of no one who has willingly encountered more perils and hardships to serve our enslaved people than you have." Tubman died in 1913.

Born a slave in Virginia around 1800, Scott was taken by his owner to Missouri in 1830 and later was sold to a military doctor named John Emerson. Over the next several years, Emerson brought Scott to Illinois, then to Wisconsin. In Wisconsin, Scott married Harriet Robinson, who also became Emerson's property. Illinois was a free state (one which did not have slavery). Wisconsin was not yet a state, but Congress had voted to make it a free territory in 1820.

In 1846, Scott and his wife sued for their freedom, based on the years they had lived in Illinois and Wisconsin where slavery was forbidden. Scott had little success in the state courts. By 1853, Emerson had died and his property, including Dred Scott, was placed in the care of his brother-in-law, John Sanford. In 1853, Scott appealed his case to the U.S. Supreme Court.

Dred Scot v. John F.A. Sanford was decided in 1857. Chief Justice Roger Taney declared that, as a slave, Scott was not a U.S. citizen and therefore had no right to sue in federal court. Going even further, however, Taney (from the slave state of Maryland) declared that Congress had no power to determine slavery in a state or territory. Angry reaction against the decision in the North helped lead to the Republican Party's victory in 1860. Congress had spent years trying to make compromises between the South and the North regarding the spread of slavery, and a very fragile peace was the result of those compromises. Taney's decision shattered that peace.

Emerson's widow, Irene, regained Scott when she married a Massachusetts congressman who opposed slavery. She decided to give the Scotts back to the sons of Scott's original owner, who gave the Scotts their freedom in May 1857. Dred Scott was finally free, but had very little time to enjoy it. He died the next year.

Chief Justice Roger Taney (above) ruled against Dred Scott (right) and stated that Congress could not determine slavery in individual states. The Dred Scott decision hastened the outbreak of the Civil War.

Born in Connecticut in 1800, John Brown was raised in a strongly religious and abolitionist household. He married Dianthe Lusk in 1820, and they had seven children before she died in 1831. The next year Brown married sixteen-year-old Mary Anne Day, with whom he had thirteen more children. A failed businessman, at the age of thirty-seven Brown turned his opposition to slavery into a crusade. Brown believed that God had appointed him to end slavery.

In 1848, Brown moved to Kansas, which had been the site of violence between abolitionists and people who supported slavery. Brown and some of his sons fought on the side of the abolitionists in what became known as "bleeding Kansas." Brown was responsible for the deaths of a number of men, especially at Pottawatomie, a small proslavery settlement, where he and his followers hacked five men to death with

This illustration depicts the execution of John Brown. His death moved many northerners to join the fight against slavery.

swords. After the death of one of his sons, Brown swore, "I will die fighting for this cause. There will be no more peace in this land until slavery is done for."

Brown moved back to the East in 1856 and began to raise money to create a slave revolt. On October 16, 1859, he led a group of twenty men, including five blacks, in an attack on the federal armory and arsenal at Harpers Ferry in Virginia. Brown hoped that slaves who heard of the attack would rise up and join him in freedom. In fact, few slaves heard of the action, and none rose up. Instead, a company of marines led by Colonel Robert E. Lee surrounded Brown and his men. Ten of Brown's followers, which included two of his sons, were killed, and an injured Brown was captured.

Brown's trial took place under heavy guard. Convicted of treason, murder, and the attempt to inspire a slave revolt, Brown was hanged on December 2, 1859. To the South, he represented one of their deepest fears: the possibility of an armed slave uprising. To many in the North, he was a symbol of the fight against slavery. The death of John Brown pushed the North and South farther apart than ever.

Brown was a staunch abolitionist who fought violently for the cause.

ABRAHAM LINCOLN

HIS LEADERSHIP SAVED THE UNION

Abraham Lincoln was born in Kentucky in 1809. His mother died when he was nine years old. His stepmother taught him to read and write and he became an avid reader. With very little formal schooling, he was almost entirely self-educated. Eventually, he decided to pursue a political career and won a seat in the Illinois legislature in 1834. In 1843, Lincoln married Mary Todd, and in 1846, Lincoln was elected to the U.S. House of Representatives.

By 1860, Lincoln had become a nationally recognized figure who had argued strongly against the spread of slavery into any areas that were not yet states. The newly formed Republican Party chose him as its candidate for president that year. Lincoln won and became the nation's sixteenth president.

Because President Abraham Lincoln (opposite) was inexperienced in military matters, he appointed generals to lead the Union army in the great battles of the Civil War (above).

Many in the South feared that Lincoln would end slavery completely. Seven states seceded from the Union and formed the Confederate States of America. Lincoln had to decide whether to abandon or maintain federal property such as forts in the seceded states. When he decided to send supplies to Fort Sumter in South Carolina, Confederate soldiers opened fire on the fort and started the Civil War. After Fort Sumter, four more states joined the Confederacy.

During the Civil War, Lincoln was faced with many problems. He had almost no military training, and many of the generals that he appointed to lead the Union armies were unsuccessful. He also had to decide why the Union was fighting. Some thought the fight was to end slavery, others only to get the South to rejoin the Union. In 1862, Lincoln issued the Emancipation Proclamation. This document freed the slaves in the Confederate states and showed people that one of the goals of the Civil War was to end slavery.

The war started badly for the North, but in 1863, Union victories at Gettysburg and Vicksburg helped turn the war in favor of the North and helped Lincoln win reelection in 1864. That same year, Lincoln found the answer to his military troubles in Ulysses S. Grant, the Union general who had conquered Vicksburg. With Grant in control, the Union defeated the Confederacy in 1865.

When the war ended, Lincoln was faced with how to deal with the South. He wanted the nation to heal as quickly as possible once the fighting ended. He was still considering how to achieve this when he attended a play at Ford's Theater in Washington with his wife on April 14, 1865. That night, he was shot by John Wilkes Booth; Lincoln died early the next day.

Lincoln had tried to steer a course that would allow the United States to reunite and prosper once again. Although his death made those results more difficult to achieve, in the end his leadership had saved the nation.

President Lincoln issued the Emancipation Proclamation, which called for most slaves to be freed, in 1862.

JEFFERSON DAVIS

Jefferson Davis was born in Kentucky in 1808 and raised in Mississippi, the son of a slaveowner who had fought in the American Revolution. Davis attended West Point, from which he graduated in 1828. He served in the army for seven years, and when he resigned, he married Sarah Taylor, daughter of future U.S. president Zachary Taylor. She died while on their honeymoon, and Davis returned to Mississippi, where he bought and ran a cotton plantation. In 1844, Davis was elected to the House of Representatives, and in 1845 he married Varina Banks Howell. In 1846, Davis left Congress to re-enlist in the army to fight in the Mexican War. When he returned to Mississippi, Davis was offered a seat in the U.S. Senate.

As a senator, Davis became a strong opponent of any plan to limit the spread of slavery. Davis owned hundreds of slaves whom he treated well. He believed that slavery was in the best interests of both whites and blacks.

From 1852 to 1856, Davis served as President Franklin Pierce's secretary of war. When Pierce's presidency ended, Davis was reelected to the Senate. For the next four years, Davis fought to protect slavery and states' rights. When Abraham Lincoln was elected president in 1860, many in the South believed that he would end slavery. Mississippi seceded from the Union with six other states. Davis left the Senate, and in February 1861, he was elected president of the newly formed Confederate States of America.

Davis was facing an enemy with far more people, industry, and economic strength than his Confederacy. Davis believed in the Confederate cause, and his faith helped keep Southern hopes alive. He appointed good leaders and gave them freedom to act. He also worked hard to gain support from Europe. This support, which never came through, might have forced the Union to grant the South freedom.

Left: As senator, Jefferson Davis (left) fought for slavery and states' rights. Right: Southerners gathered at Davis's inauguration (pictured) as president of the Confederate States of America.

In 1865, when the Confederate capital at Richmond, Virginia, fell, Davis fled with what was left of his government. He was captured and imprisoned. At first Davis was accused of being a part of Lincoln's assassination, but eventually he was cleared and released. After the war, he wrote two unsuccessful books about the Confederacy. Still, when Davis died, without ever having asked for or received any pardon for his role at the center of the war, he was among the most highly regarded men in the South.

Although Davis fled after the fall of the Confederacy in 1865, Union troops captured him and escorted him to a military prison.

Clarissa Harlowe Barton was born in Massachusetts on Christmas day, 1821. Her father had fought in the Revolutionary War, and Clara grew up hearing his stories about war. She was educated and intelligent, and began to teach school when she was only fifteen years old. In 1851, she moved to New Jersey and became principal of a school. Within one year, she went from teaching six to six hundred students. When the town decided that she needed a man to be her supervisor, Barton resigned and moved to Washington, D.C.

There, she became a clerk in the Patent Office and one of the first women to work in the U.S. government. When the Civil War began, Barton began to collect food and medical supplies for Massachusetts soldiers who were staying in Washington. Soon she began to use wagons to bring her supplies to soldiers in the field. In 1862, she arrived at the battle of Antietam and began to treat the wounded while the battle still raged. One bullet passed through her sleeve and killed the

At the Battle of Antietam (pictured), Clara Barton joined soldiers in the midst of battle and began to tend to the wounded.

soldier she was working on. At Antietam, Barton earned the nickname "the Angel of the Battlefield." Though Barton had no formal medical training, she had nursed several family members, and assisted battlefield doctors and even perform some surgeries herself.

Barton spent the next three years traveling to battlefields to bring aid to soldiers despite objections from some people who did not want a woman so close to the fighting. As the war came to a close, Barton decided to help identify the thousands of missing soldiers who had been killed or captured without any proper record. She

Clara Barton founded the American Red Cross after she served as a nurse in the Civil War and the Franco-Prussian War.

started at Andersonville prison, a Confederate prisoner-of-war camp in Georgia, where she helped identify almost thirteen thousand dead Union soldiers. Barton also used newspapers, advertisements, and letters to help identify thousands of other missing men.

After the war, Barton traveled to Europe, where she came into contact with the International Red Cross, an organization founded in Europe and devoted to helping the victims of war and violence. Barton also served as a nurse during the Franco-Prussian War. When she returned to the United States, she founded the American Red Cross and served as its first president from 1881 until 1904. She died in Maryland in 1912.

ANDREW JOHNSON

Andrew Johnson was born to a poor family in Raleigh, North Carolina, in 1808. His father died when Andrew was four. Johnson worked as a tailor's apprentice before eventually running away to Tennessee. There, he met Eliza McCardle, whom he married in 1827. She helped him complete his education, and he soon began a career in politics.

After he served as mayor of his town and in the state legislature, Johnson was elected to the U.S. House of Representatives in 1843. After ten years in Congress, he became governor of Tennessee, then returned to Washington as a senator in 1857.

By then, tensions between North and South were high, and Johnson found himself caught in the middle. Though Tennessee was a slave state, Johnson's own region of east Tennessee did not have many slaves. Johnson favored slavery, but he did not favor breaking up the Union for any reason. In 1860, when seven Southern states voted to secede from the Union, Johnson made a speech against secession. His speech pleased Northerners and shocked Southerners, who felt betrayed by a leader of a fellow slave state.

In June 1861, Tennessee voted to join the Confederacy. Johnson chose to stay in Washington, the only senator to remain from a state in secession. He became a strong supporter of President Abraham Lincoln, and when the Union was able to recapture much of Tennessee in 1862, Lincoln made Johnson military governor of Tennessee.

In 1864, during his reelection campaign, Lincoln chose Johnson to run as his vice president. A short time after they won the election, and only days after the war had ended, Lincoln was assassinated and Johnson became the nation's seventeenth president. Johnson spent the next three years battling Congress. He wanted the South to be allowed to return to the Union as easily as possible, but many Northerners wanted to punish the Confederates for the war. In 1867, Congress impeached, or accused, Johnson of committing "high crimes" when he fired his secretary of war. Johnson was saved from being removed from office by one vote, and he remained president until his term ended in 1868.

In 1875, Johnson became the first ex-president to serve in the Senate, but he only made one speech. He died later that year.

Although Andrew Johnson was proslavery, he opposed breaking up the Union.
He became the seventeenth president after Lincoln's assassination.

ROBERT E. LEE

GENERAL WHO LED THE CONFEDERATE ARMY

Robert E. Lee was born in 1807 in Virginia. He was the son of Henry "Light-Horse Harry" Lee, a Revolutionary War hero. In 1829, Lee graduated second in his class from West Point without ever having earned a demerit. His early military career was uneventful, and in 1831 he married Mary Custis, a great-granddaughter of Martha Washington. When war with Mexico broke out in 1846, Lee served under General Winfield Scott. From Scott, Lee learned how to direct an army with aggression and speed.

In 1861, when the Civil War began, President Abraham Lincoln offered Lee the chance to lead the U.S. armies in the field, but Lee refused to fight against Virginia. Instead, he became a general for the Confederacy. At first, he served as military advisor to Confederate president Jefferson Davis, but when Confederate general Joseph Johnston was wounded in 1862, Lee took over. In a series of battles called the Seven Days, Lee managed to push the Union's overwhelming force away from Richmond.

Over the next three years, Lee used his usually outnumbered troops effectively and aggressively. In several instances, to achieve surprise, he divided his troops even when facing a larger enemy. This strategy almost caused Lee's defeat at Antietam when his orders fell into Union hands. After he crushed the Union army at Fredericksburg, at the end of 1862, Lee again divided his forces at Chancellorsville in 1863 and defeated a larger Union army.

Lee followed Chancellorsville with his second invasion of the North, but at Gettysburg the Confederates were defeated and forced to withdraw after heavy losses. In 1864, the Union brought General Ulysses S. Grant to face Lee. Aware that he had far more men than Lee, Grant pursued Lee's army without pause for the next year. Although Lee actually won several battles, the sheer numbers of Union soldiers overpowered his forces. After one final campaign, Lee surrendered to Grant at Appomattox Court House on April 9, 1865.

Lee had held off the Union forces for almost three years despite being outnumbered in almost every battle. At the times when things looked worst for the Confederacy, Lee gave Southerners hope and courage. After the war, Lee accepted a position as president of Washington College (today Washington and Lee University), which he ran with great success. Lee died in 1870, one of the most beloved men in the South.

Confederate general Robert E. Lee was a brilliant military strategist. Despite being outnumbered in many battles, Lee's army still fought off Union troops.

ULYSSES S. GRANT

UNION GENERAL AND U.S. PRESIDENT

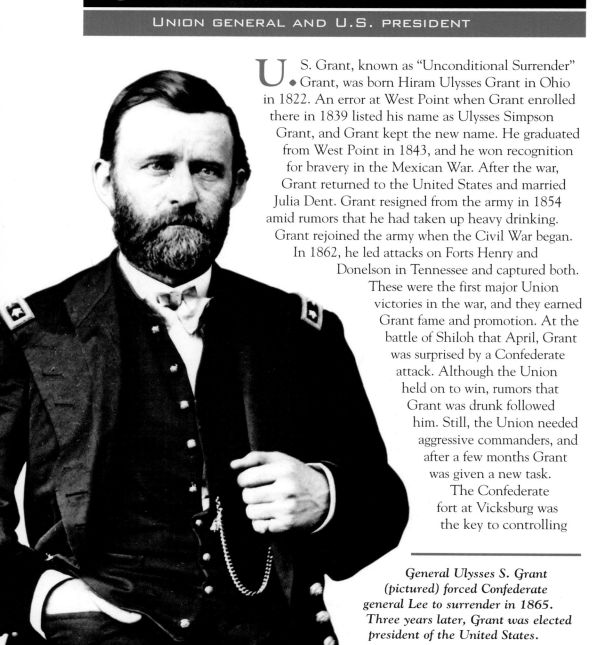

U.S. Grant, known as "Unconditional Surrender" Grant, was born Hiram Ulysses Grant in Ohio in 1822. An error at West Point when Grant enrolled there in 1839 listed his name as Ulysses Simpson Grant, and Grant kept the new name. He graduated from West Point in 1843, and he won recognition for bravery in the Mexican War. After the war, Grant returned to the United States and married Julia Dent. Grant resigned from the army in 1854 amid rumors that he had taken up heavy drinking. Grant rejoined the army when the Civil War began. In 1862, he led attacks on Forts Henry and Donelson in Tennessee and captured both. These were the first major Union victories in the war, and they earned Grant fame and promotion. At the battle of Shiloh that April, Grant was surprised by a Confederate attack. Although the Union held on to win, rumors that Grant was drunk followed him. Still, the Union needed aggressive commanders, and after a few months Grant was given a new task.

The Confederate fort at Vicksburg was the key to controlling

General Ulysses S. Grant (pictured) forced Confederate general Lee to surrender in 1865. Three years later, Grant was elected president of the United States.

General Grant (center) became known for his aggressive fighting as he led the Union army to many victories during the Civil War.

the Mississippi River and cutting off the Confederacy's flow of supplies from the West. After several failed attempts, Grant used an aggressive and creative plan to isolate and surround Vicksburg, whose thirty thousand men surrendered to him on July 4, 1863.

Soon after, Grant was promoted to lieutenant general (the first U.S. lieutenant general since George Washington) and brought east. Grant ordered all Union armies to go on the offensive in May; Grant himself led the fight against Confederate general Robert E. Lee in Virginia.

Grant knew that the Union had more men and supplies than the Confederates, and he used this advantage to the fullest. He led his own armies on a bloody chase of Lee throughout Virginia. He also ordered Union general William T. Sherman to march his army through Georgia and South Carolina. Sherman's army destroyed Southern property as it went, which helped break Confederate morale. After one final battle at Appomattox, Virginia, Grant forced Lee to surrender, and the Civil War ended. Grant's aggressive fighting helped win the Civil War and preserve the Union.

After the war, Grant was made a full general (the first in the nation's history), and in 1868, he was elected president. His two terms were marked by scandals and by trouble with the reconstruction of the South. Grant died of cancer in 1885.

Born in 1824 in what is now West Virginia, Thomas "Stonewall" Jackson was orphaned at a young age and raised in poverty. Jackson's young life was marked by a passion for education and for religion. At West Point, which he entered in 1842, Jackson had to work hard to make up for a lack of formal schooling. He graduated in the top half of his class in 1846, just in time to enter the Mexican War. After the war, Jackson accepted a teaching position at Virginia Military Institute. In 1853, Jackson got married, but his wife died during childbirth. Four years later, he married Mary Anna Morrison.

Above: "Stonewall" Jackson's troops accidentally opened fire on the general at the Battle of Chancellorsville. Opposite: A military man for his entire adult life, Jackson was known as a demanding general who pushed his troops to unlikely victories.

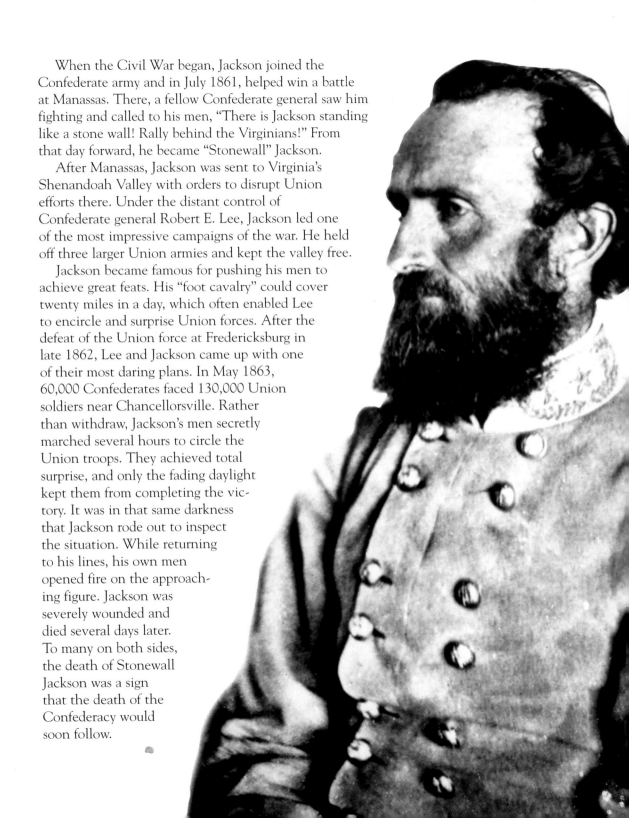

When the Civil War began, Jackson joined the Confederate army and in July 1861, helped win a battle at Manassas. There, a fellow Confederate general saw him fighting and called to his men, "There is Jackson standing like a stone wall! Rally behind the Virginians!" From that day forward, he became "Stonewall" Jackson.

After Manassas, Jackson was sent to Virginia's Shenandoah Valley with orders to disrupt Union efforts there. Under the distant control of Confederate general Robert E. Lee, Jackson led one of the most impressive campaigns of the war. He held off three larger Union armies and kept the valley free.

Jackson became famous for pushing his men to achieve great feats. His "foot cavalry" could cover twenty miles in a day, which often enabled Lee to encircle and surprise Union forces. After the defeat of the Union force at Fredericksburg in late 1862, Lee and Jackson came up with one of their most daring plans. In May 1863, 60,000 Confederates faced 130,000 Union soldiers near Chancellorsville. Rather than withdraw, Jackson's men secretly marched several hours to circle the Union troops. They achieved total surprise, and only the fading daylight kept them from completing the vic- tory. It was in that same darkness that Jackson rode out to inspect the situation. While returning to his lines, his own men opened fire on the approach- ing figure. Jackson was severely wounded and died several days later. To many on both sides, the death of Stonewall Jackson was a sign that the death of the Confederacy would soon follow.

Born in Ohio in 1820, William T. Sherman was raised by a foster family after the death of his father in 1829. He entered West Point in 1836, and in 1840 he graduated near the top of his class. He served in California during the Mexican War, and in 1850, married Ellen Ewing. In 1853 he resigned from the military to take a job as a bank manager. In 1859 he became superintendent of the Louisiana Military Seminary. When Louisiana voted to secede in 1861, Sherman left and returned north.

Sherman reenlisted in the army and in August he was ordered to command Union troops in Kentucky. There, he was accused of panicking and overestimating the Confederate forces. He was labeled insane in the newspapers, and removed from command after only a few months. After a brief absence, Sherman participated in the defeats of Forts Henry and Donelson, where he met Union general Ulysses S. Grant.

After more success at Shiloh, Sherman was promoted to major general. He served with Grant and helped to win battles at Vicksburg, Mississippi, and at Chattanooga and Knoxville, Tennessee. In 1864, when Grant was named overall Union commander, Sherman was placed in charge of all the armies of the west. Together, he and Grant planned the final phase of the war.

In September, Sherman captured Atlanta, Georgia, evacuated the city, and burned everything that had military value. Then he began his March to the Sea, to Savannah, Georgia, with his sixty thousand troops. Along the way, they left a huge path of destruction. Sherman hoped that by destroying property, he could break the will of the South and convince it to surrender.

Sherman captured Savannah on December 23, and sent President Abraham Lincoln a telegram that presented the city as a Christmas gift. From there, Sherman turned north into South Carolina, where he continued the destruction. Eight days after Confederate Robert E. Lee surrendered to Grant in Virginia, the last Confederate army surrendered to Sherman in North Carolina.

After the war, Sherman became the army commander when Grant was elected president in 1868. He retired in 1883. Although Sherman was despised throughout the South because of his destructive march, he is credited for helping to end the war, and his ideas of destruction as a military tool remain influential today.

In order to convince the weakened Confederacy to surrender, William Tecumseh Sherman set fire to Atlanta and led Union troops on a path of destruction through Georgia.

Born in New York around 1823, Mathew Brady suffered an eye affliction that eventually left him almost blind. Interested in art from an early age, Brady met Samuel F. B. Morse when Brady was young. Morse, who had invented the telegraph, was a painter and photographer who made what were called daguerreotypes, an early form of photography.

Brady learned the elements of photography from Morse, and became a portrait photographer. He opened his own studios in New York and Washington, D.C. Brady made portraits of several famous Americans, and soon he employed dozens of photographers.

Opposite: Mathew Brady devoted himself to battlefield photography during the Civil War. Above: Brady's photographers took this picture of a photographer's camp on the battlefield in Virginia.

When the Civil War began, Brady decided to devote his studios' efforts to recording that war. The idea of battlefield photography was still very new. One problem was that it took a long time for an image to form, so no action shots were possible. Instead, Brady's photographers traveled with the Union army and took portrait shots of soldiers and officers, or photos of battlefields after a battle. Although Brady is credited with thousands of photographs during the war, almost all of them were taken by his employees, since his eyesight had worsened.

When the magazine *Harper's Weekly* published a series of photographs taken by Brady's employee Alexander Gardner after a battle at Antietam, many Northerners were shocked by the visible horror of war. It was the first time that anyone in America had ever seen a photograph of dead men on a battlefield. The photographs helped stir up support for the war by some, and opposition to the war by others. Throughout America and in Europe, the most memorable images of the American Civil War came from Brady's photographers.

Brady died in 1896. His images helped describe and define the Civil War to the people of his own time and to generations who came after.

CHRONOLOGY

1846–1848	U.S. War with Mexico; many future U.S. Civil War generals gain significant combat experience.
1857	Supreme Court rules against Congress's right to limit slavery in Dred Scott v. John F.A. Sanford.
October 1859	John Brown leads antislavery raid in Harpers Ferry, Virginia. Brown is captured and hanged in December.
November 1860	Abraham Lincoln, Republican, is elected U.S. president.
December 1860	South Carolina becomes the first Southern state to secede from the Union.
February 1861	Seven Southern states that had seceded form the Confederate States of America. Jefferson Davis is selected as president.
April 1861	Confederate forces fire on Union's Fort Sumter in Charleston, South Carolina, and the Civil War begins.
July 1861	Union forces defeated at the battle of Bull Run (or Manassas) in Virginia, the first major battle of the war.
April 1862	Battle of Shiloh in Tennessee brings highest casualties in the war up to that date.
September 1862	Union forces push back Confederate invasion of Maryland at the battle of Antietam in the war's bloodiest day.
December 1862	Union suffers massive casualties at the battle of Fredericksburg in Virginia.
January 1862	Lincoln's Emancipation Proclamation goes into effect, declaring freedom for all slaves in Confederate territories.
May 1863	Confederates defeat Union forces at Chancellorsville in Virginia; Stonewall Jackson is killed.
July 1–3, 1863	Confederate invasion of Pennsylvania is stopped at the battle of Gettysburg, which results in more casualties than any other battle of the war.
July 4, 1863	Ulysses S. Grant leads Union capture of Vicksburg, Mississippi, splitting the Mississippi River (and the Confederacy) in two.

This engraving of General Sherman's March to the Sea depicts the destruction wrought during the Civil War. In the years that followed, the country would face the massive task of rebuilding.

March 1864	Grant appointed overall Union commander by President Lincoln.
May–July, 1864	Grant's army marches into Virginia and begins a series of bloody battles with Lee's forces.
September 1864	General William Tecumseh Sherman captures Atlanta, Georgia. Sherman begins his March to the Sea.
Late 1864	Sherman burns a path through Georgia, reaching Savannah at Christmas.
January 1865	Sherman turns north and marches into South Carolina; begins to chase Lee's army.
April 1865	Confederate capital Richmond falls to Union forces. Lee surrenders to Grant at Appomattox. Lincoln is assassinated a few days later.

For Further Information

Books

Catherine Clinton, *Scholastic Encyclopedia of the Civil War*. New York: Scholastic, 1999.

Kathlyn Gay and Martin Gay, *Voices form the Past: Civil War*. New York: Twenty-First Century, 1995.

David S. Heidler and Jeanne T. Heidler, eds., *Encyclopedia of the American Civil War*. New York: W.W. Norton, 2000.

Chris Hughes, *Battlefields Across America: Antietam*. Brookfield, CT: Twenty-First Century, 1998.

—, *Battlefields Across America: Gettysburg*. Brookfield, CT: Twenty-First Century, 1998.

—, *The Battle of Antietam*. San Diego, CT: Blackbirch, 2001.

—, *Stonewall Jackson*. San Diego, CT: Blackbirch, 2001.

James M. McPherson, *The Atlas of the Civil War*. New York: MacMillan, 1994.

Stewart Sufakis, *Who Was Who in the Civil War*. New York: Facts On File, 1988.

About The Author

Chris Hughes holds a B.A. in history from Lafayette College and an M.A. in social studies education from Lehigh University. A history teacher and school administrator, Hughes teaches both U.S. and world history and has written several books on the American Civil War and on developing nations. Hughes currently lives and works at a boarding school in Chatham, Virginia, with his wife, Farida, and their children, Jordan and Leah.

⊚ FOR FURTHER INFORMATION

WEBSITES

The American Civil War Homepage
http://sunsite.utk.edu/civil-war/
A huge site with images, time lines, biographies, history, and detailed information on troops, battles, and genealogies.

Civil War Biographies
http://webpages.marshall.edu/~hughes11/biographies.htm
Links to biographies of over forty major figures in and around the time of the Civil War.

Civil War Biographies
www.civilwarhome.com
Part of the Home of the American Civil War website, this has links to biographies and images of more than one hundred figures central to the period of the Civil War.

The Civil War
www.pbs.org
The site for Ken Burns's PBS film on the Civil War, including excellent historical and biographical information, images, maps, battle details, and key documents.

Life Stories of Civil War Heroes
www.geocities.com
Biographies and links for six significant but lesser-known figures in the Civil War.

Women of the American Civil War
http://americancivilwar.com
Biographies and images of thirteen important women during the Civil War era. Part of http://americancivilwar.com, another huge and varied site with links to resources on all aspects of the war.